The Nature of Being

Joseph P. Kauffman

this book is a collection of writings that i have written over the years. some were written in my journals while traveling or on retreat, others when i was feeling lost and trying to remind myself of the joy and beauty of life, and some when i was filled with love inspiring me to help others to find happiness and freedom.

all of these writings have a common theme: coming home to the present moment, and allowing ourselves to experience the freedom of being our natural selves. the mind can often cause great disturbance and suffering, but if we can reconnect with the truth of who we are, the awareness beyond the mind, and the love within our hearts, then we can rest as this loving awareness and be at peace.

there is no specific order to the writings, so feel free to flip through the pages and read whatever you feel called to. some of the writings may seem repetitive, or contradictory to what is written in other writings, but they are as they are, and each was written as a verbal expression of a significant experience or of realizations during my personal journey of life, so i feel no need to alter them or modify them in any way. may you find what benefits you, and leave behind what does not.

may the words in this book remind you of the peace that is inherent within you.
may you awaken to this peace within, and
may you share this peace with the world.

nothing to do,

no place to go,

nothing happening but this.

there is beauty all around us,

but if we are distracted by the mind and it's fantasies

we will never see it.

calm your mind.

let go of the need to do something.

let go of the need to figure things out.

let go of the need to fill this moment with something
else.

stop creating problems for yourself.

let go.

relax.

open yourself to what is here.

just be where you are.

be as you are.

this is enough.

distinguish your social mind and social identity
from your natural mind and natural awareness.

the journey of awakening is the journey within.
it may help to have peaceful surroundings and a
supportive community, but ultimately it is not
dependent on that.
it is dependent on you and your willingness to look
deeply and honestly within yourself.
who are you really?
what is the nature of the mind,
of the universe, of life?
what prevents you from living in love, from being
open to life, from trusting and surrendering to the
unknown experience of each moment?
what keeps you in fear?
what prevents you from being here fully?
only you can awaken yourself, just as it is only you
that keeps you in delusion and ignorance.
the essence of wisdom is awareness, seeing things
clearly as they are, not how the mind labels them.
observe the mind and its habitual patterns, its endless
cycles of thought, and discover what is beyond it.
let go of the mental noise that veils you from reality.
be aware of this moment.
open your heart to all that is.

what a trip the mind can be!
it engages, it reacts, it clings,
it cries and worries,
complains and resists,
it gets upset and frustrated,
excited and impatient,
it contemplates and thinks,
it imagines and plans,
it jumps back and forth, up and down,
running around, story-telling,
fantasizing, judging, labeling,
ever-active and restless,
and i am at the mercy of this wild animal going for a
ride wherever it takes me.
that is until i look, with whole-hearted attention, at
this active mind.
where is it?
it is nowhere to be found.
as soon as i look for it, it disappears.
it is like a ghost, a phantom, an apparition.
upon observation, there is no mind, no thought, no
"i," no "me," just the observing presence.
seeing this i laugh!
i let go.
i exhale a sigh of relief and i bask in this present
moment.

there is no suffering but in the mind and our
unwillingness to observe it.
ignorantly we identify with it and it takes us on many
journeys.
it searches endlessly for peace, yet it is the very thing
that disturbs it.
in forgetfulness, we become it's slave.
in awareness, we remember our freedom.
may i stray from the present moment no longer.
may i remember that peace is here.
all i need is within me.
there is nothing to gain or lose.
great is the joy of a simple life,
endless the peace of a silent mind.
blissful is the feeling of an open heart,
that knows it's love is divine.

i feel as though i have discovered a great secret to peace and joy.

most of us have the subconscious belief that we need something else to make us happy.

we don't feel complete.

we feel like something is missing.

and so we try to fill that inner void with external objects.

we imagine some future goal, some object we want, some task we want to accomplish, some job or relationship that we long for, and then, once we finally fulfill that desire, we can at last be happy.

many of us do this repeatedly, and yet fail to realize that the object of our desire never brings us real fulfillment, and so we just keep on seeking.

maybe the next desire will do it, or the next, and so on.

if we took a moment to inquire into this, we would discover that there really is nothing outside of us that can bring us lasting peace.

the nature of life is to change, and either the object of our desire changes, or our emotions towards that object change.

when we seek for something permanent in what is inherently impermanent, we are bound to suffer.

so what is this secret to peace and joy?

renounce.

renounce the desire to find peace in the world.

this doesn't mean to renounce the world itself, or to be a monk and head for the himalayas.

it means to renounce from the mind any ideas of gaining something "out there" that will bring happiness to what is "in here."

this is only really possible when we see the truth that there is no true joy to be found "out there," but that peace, happiness, and joy are inherent within us.

it is because of our constant seeking that we create stress and disturbance for ourselves.

the secret to peace is to just be where you are, to be content with what is here.

when we renounce all expectations of gain, and all desires of how things "should be," we can enjoy how they truly are.

we can allow everything to be as it is, without trying to control it or change it in anyway, because we see the truth that happiness is right here within us.

so let come what comes, let go what goes, and remain present and grounded within yourself.

when you don't want anything from anyone, when you aren't seeking to get something out of every situation, or to get one up on life, you can just relax and enjoy.

when the mind is quiet, the heart opens to life.

the mind is always trying to figure things out.
it seeks to grasp things intellectually, to define them,
to label them, and to put them into some conceptual
category.
we can create much stress for ourselves by trying to
figure everything out in this way—trying to figure out
our path, our future, our life.
all of this takes us away from being here,
in this moment,
which is the only moment we can truly live in.

be okay with not knowing.
have patience and trust.
allow things to take their course,
and to fall into place naturally.
if you can accept that the future is ultimately
unknowable anyway, you can relax into the present.
and when you are relaxed in this moment, not seeking
to be anywhere else, but content just to be here, then
peace is available to you.

the mind is the source of all disturbance,
for it grasps and rejects experience,
attempting to define what is ultimately undefinable.
we can know reality, but only by being it.
relax the mind.
be still.
be empty.
allow reality to reveal itself.
allow your true nature to be as it is:
natural awareness, open and free.

because of our conditioning in this society, and our
need to relate and interact socially, we have developed
a social identity, with social roles, and a social
image—all of which help us to relate to others
socially.
unfortunately, many of us confuse these social
constructs with the reality of who we are.
we really believe ourselves to be this social identity,
with its name, its accomplishments, its reputation, its
culture, its education, its career, its inner self-talk,
thoughts, and so on.
but this is not the reality of who we are.
as the old zen koan asks:
"what is your original face?"
what is the truth of your being—beyond this social
matrix of thoughts, beliefs, stories, education, and
conditioning?

the mind is a living thing.
it is constantly moving,
and if we are to understand it,
we need to constantly watch its movements,
 moment to moment.
we must move with it,
be aware of its patterns,
and see how it reacts to different situations and
circumstances.
the language of our culture has conditioned us to see
things in a certain way.
the word "mind" is a noun, implying that the mind is
a static thing.
but in reality there are no "nouns," as everything is
constantly changing.
everything is an event, a verb, a process.
we tend to think of our "self" as a static and
unchanging thing as well,
but just as anything else we are alive, impermanent,
and constantly changing from moment to moment.
language reflects the beliefs and worldview of the
culture that created it,
and without realizing it,
we are under the spell of language,
hypnotized by words and programmed by culture to
perceive the world in a particular way.

the only way to be free of this conditioning,
and to see reality as it truly is,
is to be aware of the living moment,
without imposing any of our learned concepts,
judgments and beliefs onto it.
fresh, undefined, direct experience—
pure awareness of what is—
that is how we see clearly,
and when we are fully open and awake to this ever
changing moment,
we are in touch with life,
and are able to adapt to circumstances with great ease,
because mentally, we don't resist what happens,
so emotionally, we are content with whatever arises.
to be able to experience life without judging it,
labeling it, or attempting to define it,
but simply living it freely, and being one with the
whole movement of life,
this is the source of great wisdom, deep peace, and
incredible freedom.

we mistakenly identify with the mind,
and believe ourselves to be the thinker with all of its
problems.
realize that you are not the thinker,
but the seer of thought,
the space within which all exists.

let go of the disturbing thoughts and be free.
be here,
feel the energy around and within.
rest in your natural state.

abiding calmly and stably in your own nature,
you are present to all of life,
open to everything,
intimate with each changing moment.
ever present, ever free, no longer bound by the mind
and it's concepts;
content and at peace within yourself.
this is enough.

what allows one to reach greater states of
consciousness?
a greater commitment to inner observation.
when spiritual practice becomes an endless practice.
when you have the devotion to give up everything for
the sake of truth.
surrender every thought to that presence from which
thought arises.
trust in the greater intelligence that moves through all.
continually let go of the mind's stories about reality,
and experience reality as it is.
the mind is always seeking to get one up on the next
moment, to get an advantage on experience, and in
doing so, it believes it knows better than that great
intelligence of nature.
surrender the ego's need to get one up on life,
and experience the totality of life as it is lived
in each moment.

the thought of "i" or "me," with all of its memories,
desires, hopes, fears, and fantasies,
is a product of the mind, and in mistakenly identifying
ourselves with this mind-made entity,
we feel that we have to constantly validate ourselves
by protecting and improving our self-image.
because of our obsession with this self-image, we are
full of anxiety, full of fear, full of greed, and we are
consumed by a continuous feed of random and
unnecessary thoughts for a majority of our lives—all
just to maintain an illusion, all to protect a self that
has no basis in reality, a self that feels it is alone,
isolated, and separate from the rest of existence.
if we were able to observe this within us—not merely
at the intellectual level, but at the actual level, the
experiential level—then we would see clearly that we
are not the mind-entity, we are the living being, the
awareness that is able to witness this mental process.

in realizing our true nature as awareness, as a living
being, we can let go of our attachment to the
psychological image of self that we have mistakenly
perceived ourselves to be.

in doing so, we can also let go of all the fears, all the
obsession, and all the confused and egocentric
motives that are attached to this illusory self, and we
can discover our inherent freedom, the inherent peace
and joy of being alive, and our inherent oneness with
all living beings.

when we see our oneness with the whole of life, love
and compassion naturally arises within us. when we
let go of our obsession with the psychological self, we
begin to truly care for others, and we are inspired to
be of service to others, and to act in ways that benefit
all living beings.

when you see the world as yourself, self-interest takes
on a whole new meaning,
and out of love, you want to serve the whole that you
are a part of.

this is what the world needs—people who have
awaken to the truth of who they are, become free of
their ego-identification and the suffering caused by it,
and who, out of love and compassion, have a sincere
wish to serve others and work for the benefit of all
living beings.

it's important to make time for yourself just to be—
to have no plans,
no task to accomplish,
nothing to do.
just be.
take a break from the hustle,
from the stress,
from all of the mental strain.
put it all aside,
and just relax.
sit outside.
feel the wind.
smell the air.
listen to the sounds of nature.
give yourself the time and space to reconnect with
yourself.
no mask to put on, no role to play.
just be yourself,
breathing,
being as you are.
make time to cultivate your inner peace,
so you can bring this peace
into the activities of your daily life.

instead of judging the appearance of your body, why
not appreciate the incredible miracle that it is?
your body is an expression of the whole universe,
in which all the forces of nature are present.
it is composed of trillions of atoms,
billions of cells,
and numerous biological systems that are all working
harmoniously every single moment to keep you alive.
your body is what allows you to be here
and to experience the miracle of life.
you are a vessel in which the universe has become
conscious of itself!
everything about you is nothing shy of miraculous.
don't let society's ridiculous standards distract you
from appreciating the beautiful being
that you truly are.
appreciate this body,
appreciate existence,
appreciate everything and everyone
in this precious and mysterious life.

everything in nature grows according to simple
mathematical patterns—from stars and galaxies, to
humans and animals.
once you are aware of the geometry in nature, you'll
begin to see it everywhere.
the things that seem to be intricate and complex,
when observed closer,
reveal the simple order and intelligence of nature.
seeing these patterns in nature and in my own body
reminds me that i am part of a greater whole.
each one of us is the whole of nature expressing itself
in the form of a human being,
 like individual branches
stemming from a single tree.
how amazing!

we so easily lose our peace by stressing about the
future, or feeling ashamed of something that
happened in the past.
it's easy to get lost in planning, fantasizing,
desiring, etc. but when we do this, we only forget the
beauty of life as it is right here and now.
i know you have plans, goals, and dreams to work
toward.
but enjoy the process.
don't rush through life and overlook the magic of it
all.
you are alive.
you get to experience this mysterious universe, full of
color, sensation, and activity.
you get to participate in this incredible phenomenon
that is life!
you were born in a human body, one of the most
magnificent and intricate things the universe has ever
produced.
you have the freedom to play, to have fun, and dance
with this cosmic symphony.
rejoice!
life is beautiful!
you are beautiful!
if you are stressed out and anxious, just put those
thoughts on pause for a moment and focus on what
you are grateful for.
gratitude always creates a better attitude.
may you realize the beauty of life here and now.

observe your mind,
become aware of the content of your mind—
the thoughts, the habits, the impulses,
the desires, the conditioning.
inquire into the source of these mental objects and
ask yourself if they are necessary.
notice how many thoughts just bring us suffering—
thoughts of fear, thoughts of doubt, thoughts of
shame, judgment, anger, guilt, regret, etc.
we create the content in our minds—mostly out of
unawareness—and we can choose what we agree with
or disagree with, and thus what thoughts we empower
and disempower.
a thought only has power over you if you believe in it.
don't believe in the mental chatter.
instead, just observe it and let it come and go on its
own accord.
the more you relax as the observer, and the more you
consciously choose to think positively, the more
peaceful your mind will become.

the mind is like a garden.
thoughts are like seeds.
we can plant seeds of happiness,
or seeds of sadness,
seeds of love and appreciation,
or seeds of fear and desire.
you are the gardener.
what seeds will grow are the seeds
that you water with your attention.

realize the limitations of mind.
the mind functions through language,
images, and concepts.
these are representations of reality,
but they are not reality itself.
the mind creates stories of reality,
but is incapable of knowing reality in its essence.
only awareness can be attentive
to the true reality of here and now.
mind is simply the commentator.
at times a commentator is useful,
but they are never able to describe
any moment in its entirety,
only fractions of the moment,
filtered through personal opinion.
don't believe in the stories of your mind.
reclaim your power by continually bringing your
attention to what is here and now.
it is in the moment that life truly exists.

we have been raised to believe that we are our body,
our thoughts, our personality, our likes and dislikes,
our beliefs, our memories, our accomplishments, our
race, our nationality, our social roles—but all of these
are just stories that we tell ourselves.
when we observe the illusory nature of these stories,
they begin to dissolve in the
ocean of our pure awareness.
this dissolution is not painful,
as the illusions were never really real in the first place.
yet, people have a tremendous sense of fear and
resistance when they believe
that they are losing something.
but life is constantly changing,
and there is no permanent form that we can cling to
and hold on to for a sense of security or identity.
nothing lasts, and eventually even this body will go.
in realizing this, we can see that our true identity is
no-identity, and we can realize the preciousness of
our existence as it is right here and now.

when we let go of our attachment to any and all
forms of identification, we stand face to face with the
great mystery of life, the unknowable and ungraspable
reality of the here and now.
fearlessly open your heart to the present moment,
and stand in this vulnerable presence to what is.
this radical openness to the mystery of life is the soil
in which the flower of love grows.
open and present to all things,
without any seeking for an identity to separate us,
we realize our unity with life and within us grows
an incredible intimacy with every living being,
and every precious moment of our experience

may you be graceful with yourself as you go through this healing journey.

understand that healing takes time.

may you be patient with yourself as you heal.

may you be kind to yourself.

may you forgive yourself for anything of the past.

may you have the courage to let go of what no longer serves you.

may you give yourself the love and attention that you seek.

it has been said before that
"heaven and hell are a tenth of an inch apart."
heaven and hell are not physical places,
but states of mind.
we can be in difficult and even painful circumstances
and still be filled with contentment and inner peace.
we can be in heaven physically,
but if we are in hell mentally,
we will experience suffering.
we can be in hell physically,
but if we are in heaven mentally,
we will experience peace.
the mind shapes our experience of reality.
heaven and hell are a matter of perception.
this is commonly an unpopular perspective among
those who live with a victim mentality, and tend to
blame circumstances as being responsible for their
happiness or unhappiness—and certainly there are
circumstances that make it more challenging to feel at
peace—but the more we investigate the inner
workings of our minds, the more we realize the truth
that perception and attitude shape our experience of
reality.
many people live in a material heaven, yet they suffer
emotionally.
many people live in a material hell, and yet they are
joyous and relaxed.

it depends upon how we interpret our circumstances,
whether we accept them or resist them, appreciate
them or neglect them, complain or make the most of
them, and to what degree of emotional intensity we
relate to them.

all that you need to live in heaven is within you
already.

it is not found in a foreign place, in material gain, or
in some relationship.

it is found within yourself.

it can be discovered here and now.

we are already in heaven,

yet many of us insist on creating a mental hell.

the more we observe ourselves honestly,

the more we will realize this to be true.

the more aware we become of our minds,

the more we will notice the limiting beliefs and
negative thought patterns within us

that shape our experience of life.

observe your mind.

see the content of your thoughts.

are they bringing you happiness or suffering?

are they even true or are they just mental opinions
that are ultimately illusory?

the sooner you stop creating hell for yourself,

the sooner you can connect with the heavenly peace
that is always present within you.

what is the cause of suffering?
according to many spiritual teachers,
suffering is caused by ignorance.
because we are ignorant of who we truly are,
we identify with a mental image of self, and we
become emotionally attached and concerned with
validating and protecting this illusory image.
so how do we awaken from this ignorance?
how do we come to know our true selves?
we awaken from ignorance through becoming aware
of that which we have been ignoring.
what is it you aren't willing to look at?
is there information that you resist and push away?
are there beliefs or views you are attached to?
are you willing to really look at yourself and your
beliefs, your motives, your thoughts, your attitude,
your worldview, the content of your mind, your
habits, your reactions, your cravings, your fears, your
emotions, your actions, your food, your environment,
how you relate to life, how you treat others, how you
live and how your life impacts your environment?
there is a lot that we resist, and a lot that we aren't
willing to look at.
with honesty, courage, and devotion to discovering
the truth, we can look.
observe yourself.
observe what arises in your mind each day.
observe your reaction to events.
observe what you attach to, what you crave,
what your intention is.

where does all this originate?

why do you seek what you seek?

what do you think it will provide you with?

observe, and ask yourself what is that observing presence?

what is it that is observing?

what is this awareness?

if "i" believe myself to be the thought of "i" or "me," along with the history, memory, and ideas attached to this concept of "i," then who is it that can observe this "i" thought?

come to know this observing presence.

be awareness itself, and witness all that arises within this awareness that you are.

this awareness is essential for all experience.

it is at the source of all life.

the awareness within you, is of the same substance as the awareness within me.

we are one, expressed as many.

seeing yourself in all, you fall in love with all.

this love for existence is the source of true happiness, freedom, and peace.

the only thing preventing us from this is the fear of really discovering what is true.

it is easy to lose ourselves in the circumstances
of our lives.
so many sensations, energies and activities are
constantly changing,
often stimulating thoughts in our minds that tend to
distract us from the simple joy of being.
remember that at any moment,
including this moment now,
you can pause, take a deep breath in, and exhale,
letting go of any tension you may be holding—
physical or mental.
the breath can bring us home to the present moment,
and in this moment,
is the only moment that we can find peace.
let go of the future worries and past regrets.
quiet the reactive thinking mind.
breathe in the energy of life.
appreciate this breath, this life, this moment.
relax your mind and be free.

can you distinguish your conditioned mind, with its
judgments, prejudices, beliefs, concepts, evaluations,
etc. from your natural awareness, which is simply
present, aware, nonjudgmental, unbiased,
unconditioned and free?
before you learned who you were, where you came
from, what life is, and so on, who were you?
has that original nature left you?
can you rediscover it, and by doing so, let go of the
mistaken belief that you are your social identity?
and can you integrate this deeper knowledge of
yourself into a society that does not socially accept
such a depth of self-understanding?
can you learn to operate from this natural self, while
still playing the social game?
and with compassion for those still caught in their
social identities, can you play this game skillfully so as
to help these beings to awaken to their true nature?

let go of the unnecessary pressure that you put on
yourself.

let go of the belief that you need anything else to be
more complete.

let go of the self-judgment and criticism.

let go of the craving for something in the future,
understanding it is only a mental fantasy taking you
away from what is right here and now.

let go of the thoughts that distract you from life,
which is always now.

let go of what does not serve you.

let go of anything that is less than love.

letting go of all unnecessary effort, all of the attempts
to grasp and control life, we can find peace within
ourselves.

do not look for peace outside of yourself.

the nature of the world is to change.

nothing is permanent.

nothing lasts.

trying to find stability and permanence in what is
inherently unstable and impermanent only results in
suffering.

things of the world are not the source of peace, nor is
there peace in the mind.

the mind is inherently restless, always thinking,
dividing reality, disturbing us.

peace is found beyond the mind.

peace is your nature, which becomes clear when the
mind is quiet.

when we surrender the unnecessary thoughts, stories,

fears, worries, concepts, beliefs, fantasies, etc. and just allow ourselves to be as we are, we find that peace is already here.

peace comes from accepting and being with what is, from being as we are, from resting in our open awareness.

when you realize peace is within your own being, you can be relaxed in any circumstance, for you are not dependent on situations and events as the source of your happiness.

be content with what is.

let go of the illusion that peace comes from anything outside of you.

it is right here and now, ever-present, and it will become known as soon as you surrender the mental disturbance that distracts you from the simple joy of being alive.

love is the source of true happiness.
not the romantic love we know of in our culture,
not the limited and selected love between a few
individuals,
but the love that comes from realizing our unity,
from seeing that we all share this existence,
that in truth there is no division between us.
when you feel another's suffering as your own,
when their happiness is your happiness,
love inspires you to serve.
the fear of the mind will be hesitant.
the ego will ask what it can gain from it.
but the heart will give and love freely.
quiet the mind.
humble the ego.
listen to the heart.
your life is an expression of the all.
all that you have has been given by nature.
how can we give back to the all and it's expressions?
how can we express our gratitude to nature
in action, word, and thought?
love inspires us to be of service,
and to serve others is the greatest joy.
their happiness, your happiness, is its own reward.
no matter what the mind says, what ego says, or what
culture says, a soft and kind heart is a blessing to all.

underneath the mental noise,

preceding any conceptual interpretation or judgment,

beyond every thought,

there is an infinite silence.

let go and relax into this silence.

feel the divinity of this ever present beingness

that you are.

you are not the thinker.

the thinker is only thoughts.

you are that space in which all things exist.

you have no form.

you have no name.

there is no way to describe yourself,

but you can be yourself,

at peace in this very moment.

i think one of the most important questions we can
ask ourselves is:
how can i awaken the love within my heart?
love is the sensation of unity that we feel with all
beings,
and when our heart is open, everyone and everything
is seen as family, is seen as our own self.
when you look at another being, what do you see?
do you create an image of them, and then feel some
kind of emotion or reaction according to your own
self-created image?
do you see the circumstances
or the body that being is in?
or do you see them as they truly are?
do you look at them as another living being, just like
you, with their own experiences, joys and hardships?
judgment and fear is what keeps us away from love.
how can we see with the eyes of love when our minds
are clouded by judgment?
if you wish to awaken the love inherent within you,
then become aware of the thoughts within your mind.
see what it is that keeps you closed off from life, and
what prevents you from accepting things as they are.
do you judge yourself as you are,
or accept yourself as you are?
are you kind or unkind to yourself?
whatever we hold within is what we project outwards,
so to discover love in the world,
first realize it within yourself.
when you awaken the love within your heart, then it

becomes impossible to harm or mistreat another,
because you no longer see any difference between you
and "other" living beings.
there is only one universal energy, that expresses itself
as each one of us.
when you realize this energy within you,
you realize that it is also within everyone and
everything else.
then love comes naturally,
and with it, joy, happiness, contentment, and peace.
as the great sufi poet rumi pointed out,

*"your task is not to seek for love, but merely to seek and find
all the barriers within yourself that you have built against it"*
for love comes naturally when our hearts are open.
but when we live in fear the heart remains closed.
look within yourself.
see what needs healing, and give it the love and
attention required to heal it.
discover that love is within you,
then you can share this love with the whole of life.

what is the root cause of misery?
what is it that causes one to suffer?
when "i" am depressed,
when "i" am anxious,
when "i" am frustrated,
when "i" am stressed,
do not all of these states apply to this "i"?
well what is this "i"?
have you ever tried to find out?
when the physical organ of the eye sees an image,
we say "i" see.
are we the eye?
when the physical ear perceives a sound,
we say "i" hear.
are we the ear?
upon investigation,
can we find this "i" anywhere in the body?
can we find where this "i" resides?
can we find what this "i" is?
"i" is just a word, a sound, a thought.
all words have been learned from our culture, from
the language we have inherited.
when this body was born, did you say or think "i"
have been born?
when this body was in the womb, were you saying or
thinking "i" am in the womb?
of course not.
the word "i" was learned.
and we have attached to this word a whole network
of concepts, words, images, and emotions, and we

relate ourselves to this network that surrounds "i."
but "i" is only a thought.
what happens when we stop identifying ourselves as
"i"?
what happens when we see that "I" has no reality
other than in the mind?
when we see that "i" is kept alive because we keep
feeding it energy?
and because it is enforced by society?
what happens when we let go of the "i" thought?
do we stop existing?
do the eyes stop seeing?
or ears stop hearing?
things continue to function on their own,
spontaneously as they always have.
in fact, they function much more organically, as the
intelligent energy of nature can express itself
authentically and freely, for there is no longer any
barriers of resistance.
when we see through the "i"
when we see it for what it is, and no longer identify as
that, what else happens?
all of the fear, all of the anxiety, all of the craving,
aversion, and suffering that came from identifying as
this "i" also drops away.
when the cause of suffering is removed, the natural
state of freedom is experienced as it is.
natural presence.
open awareness.
pure beingness.

when the one intelligent energy that is the source and
substance of all realizes itself,
it abides in the bliss of being as it is.

we never really know the circumstances
that others are experiencing.
but knowing that we have suffered,
enables us to see that others suffer just like we do.
people often hide their suffering and
look as if they are not suffering on the surface,
but deep down they may be in great pain.
knowing that everyone experiences suffering
in their own way,
and that all beings have a common desire
to be happy,
should inspire us to do our best
to free people from their suffering,
to be kind to others at all times,
because even the smallest act of kindness
can feel like a breath of fresh air
to someone who is suffocating from their suffering.

many people are looking for an escape from reality.
they look for it in drugs, in food, in sensual pleasures,
and in mental distractions of all kinds.

some even turn to spirituality as a means to help them
escape reality.

but if you are sincere in your spiritual journey you'll
realize that it isn't about escaping reality, but rather
awakening to it.

this journey of awakening is not just about positive
vibes, chakras, love, light, and rainbows—as great as
all those things are.

it is about awakening from our ignorance, becoming
free of our mental illusions and conditioning, and
learning to see and accept reality as it truly is.

this is not accomplished without some discomfort in
the healing process.

the journey of awakening invites us to look at our
shadow, to observe our minds and our habitual
patterns, and to no longer push away our feelings
because they are uncomfortable.

it teaches us how to live with awareness.

it awakens us to the responsibility we have for
ourselves and our relationship with life.

it liberates us from our suffering by helping us to
become aware of how we create our own suffering,
and how we can create our own joy and peace instead.

it is difficult to change deeply rooted patterns and
habits, to forgive and let go of our past, and to open
our hearts fully to the present moment.
it is difficult, but oh so worth it.
we will not find peace by escaping our suffering, but
by learning how to heal it and transform it.

we can never be reminded enough of the fact that we
can maintain inner peace in any circumstance.
without realizing it,
many of us invest our emotions in situations,
and allow ourselves to be affected by what happens.
yet, it is never really the situation that causes us to
suffer, but how we react to that situation.
circumstances disturb us because we allow them to—
because we give away our power to them.
when we accept circumstances as they are, and just
allow them to be without resisting them,
we create the space for peace within ourselves.
simply because our resistance to a situation creates
discomfort and tension within us.
but when we stop resisting, and just relax with what
is, the situation becomes much more tolerable.
truly, we can be at peace in any situation, but we have
to realize that peace comes from within ourselves, not
from what is outside of us.
use your breath as a tool to cultivate inner peace.
no matter what you are doing, you can turn your
attention inward and intentionally breath deep and
relaxed breaths.
in doing so, your mind will become relaxed, and you
will inwardly be at ease, regardless of what is
happening around you.

you are alive now!
breathe in that fresh life energy with gratitude.
smile at the fact that you exist.
our problems are psychological.
let them go and laugh.
embrace the reality of life here and now.
do you hear the sounds around you?
can you feel the sensations of energy moving around
everywhere, changing and dancing? everything is just
being.
allow yourself to just be.
relax, everything will be okay.

we may not always realize it, but most of us are constantly projecting our thoughts onto our direct experience of reality, believing these projections to be true, and then reacting to them, and either feeling joy or misery because of them.

we judge events as good or bad, we label people as kind or unkind, beautiful or ugly, black or white, we judge ourselves as worthy or unworthy, attractive or unattractive, and so on.

all of these labels, judgments, and stories that we create aren't the actual truth of reality.

they exist in the mind only.

notice your mind projecting onto your direct experience, and let that judgment of reality go, simply for the fact that it isn't the actual truth of reality, but is just a mental concept and illusion.

as this process usually happens without our awareness of it, just by the very act of noticing it, bringing it into awareness, and seeing it for what it is, it loses the power of our belief and we effortlessly become free of it.

the practice is simply to remain aware of the mind's projections, and not to allow yourself to forgetfully believe in them as if they were true.

the more you do this, the freer you become from the mind's fantasies and all of the misery they so often create, and the more you reunite with the immediate, living reality of the present moment.

through this awareness you reunite with your essential beingness,

the being that is beyond the mind and it's stories.
we unknowingly seek for identity in the world, in our
jobs, our nationality or culture, our accomplishments,
our titles and certificates—and in this process of
constantly seeking outward for identity, we forget our
true identity as the pure and natural being within.
let go of the mental illusions that distract you from
your real essence.
hold onto what is true, what is real, which is the truth
that you are, you exist.
be in tune with just being, being here and now, being
aware, living, and not allowing your mind to project
fantasies that disturb your peace.

no matter how many times you fall into old patterns,
break your resolutions, or fail to follow through on
your convictions, you can always start again.
each day we are born anew.
today is a new day.
start over.
begin again.
even if you are well on the path,
each moment is a new moment.
begin again.
whatever it is you want to cultivate—inner peace,
spiritual awareness, good health, positive thoughts,
kind attitude, material wealth—start today.

one of the greatest lessons i have ever learned is
simply to relax with what is.
no matter what happens, pleasant or unpleasant,
it will pass.
so just relax with it.
appreciate it while it is here if it is pleasant.
relax and know it will pass if it is unpleasant.
cultivate a relationship with the impermanent nature
of things.
let things be as they are.
let them come.
let them go.
just be here now,
present,
centered in the heart,
and relax with whatever arises.

it's easy to take all that we have for granted.
we have the tendency to seek for more, thinking that
what we are seeking will provide us with happiness.
most don't realize it is this craving for more that is
actually the cause of their misery.
if we simply acknowledge and appreciate all that we
have in this very moment, this in itself will bring us
joy and relaxation.
the more we cultivate this attitude of gratitude, the
happier we will be.
appreciate this life, this breath, this moment, the
elements that sustain you, your loved ones, yourself!
there are so many things to be grateful for, and when
we take a moment to sincerely appreciate our
existence, then happiness and peace is sure to follow.

we cannot continue to exist with so much violence,
so much disrespect,
so much fear and judgment toward others;
we are only hurting ourselves by doing this.
our actions ripple out into the universe,
creating a chain of events that affects
every single particle in existence.
actions driven by love benefit more than just us
or those in direct contact with our actions,
they benefit the whole of existence.
any actions that are driven by fear, violence, anger,
hatred, jealousy, or greed, are produced by a mind
that is dominated by ego and selfish motives.
if we realized our connection to one another
and to the source of all life,
we would act only in love,
always having the health of life as a whole in mind.
in order to feel the love that comes
from understanding our oneness,
we have to let go of the idea that we are separate.
we have to see clearly that we are not the ego.
the ego is just a thought that the brain,
and by extension the universe, is having.

we have many ideas about life, about ourselves, about what's going in the world, about our personal circumstances.

we run through these ideas day after day, we project them onto our experiences, we suffer or enjoy events because of them.

surrender all of these ideas.

let go of everything you've been thinking about or stressing over.

release every concern.

allow yourself just a moment,

a moment to appreciate the fact that you exist.

you are a living energy.

you are alive!

you are already more than enough.

in this constantly changing reality, nothing is permanent.

but today, you are here.

you are alive now.

the whole world is yours to experience.

appreciate this moment.

appreciate this Breath.

appreciate this existence.

let go of all the useless stresses and worries.

remember what is truly important.

surrender your ideas of this day, this experience, this moment,

and open yourself to its immediate reality.

what a miracle it is to be alive.

may you appreciate this day.
may you enjoy this day.
may you be happy and peaceful
on this precious day alive.

we think that because we have invested so much of our lives in learning concepts, definitions, and beliefs about reality, that we actually know what reality is. but this is superficial knowledge.

we see a tree and we label it as "tree" thinking we already know everything there is to know about it. but if we take the time to really sit with the tree and be present with it, we will discover infinite worlds of magic and life hidden within this beautiful expression of nature, things that weren't available to us when we confined the tree to the label and concept of "tree." our minds are so quick to label, define, and judge.

we think that we know, but when we label or define anything, we only block ourselves off from discovering everything that it really is, we prevent ourselves from discovering the mysterious universe that exists just outside of our concepts and social conventions.

not many of us are aware
of just how powerful our words are.
words are energy,
and the power of speech is able to create worlds,
liberate minds, or destroy lives.
when we are aware, we can use our speech to help
rather than harm the lives of those we interact with.
our society would likely collapse
without the use of words or language.
words allow us to communicate to each other
messages from within.
with words, we can complement someone
and let them know how beautiful they are,
how special they are, and how valuable they are.
we can also put them down, make fun of them,
and tell them that they are worthless.
whether we want to use our speech for love,
or for violence,
is up to us,
but regardless,
every word that we speak has tremendous power.

we are all aware to some extent of the destruction we
are causing to this sacred living earth.

but are we aware of the ways in which we
personally contribute to this destruction?

are we willing to look at our own lifestyles and actions
to see where we are contributing to the harm of the
planet?

and are we willing to change our harmful actions and
do our best to be a human being that truly cares to be
of benefit to the whole?

can we acknowledge the self-obsession, the self-
interest, and self-grasping qualities within us—the
tendencies that cause us to focus solely on personal
gain, and to be insensitive to the whole?

the majority of human beings living today feel like
they are separate from their environment, but this
could not be further from the truth.

your body is an ecosystem in its own right, composed
of trillions of living cells, bacteria, and other
organisms, that depend upon nature's elements for
their survival.

there really isn't a line that separates you from your
environment.

the divide lies solely in our perception, in the
unexamined beliefs we have inherited from our
culture.

if we can recognize our essential unity with the whole
of nature, and are willing to be of benefit to the whole
that we are inseparable from, then we must ask
ourselves—how are my actions affecting the whole?
if success or failure of this planet and of human
beings depended on how i am and what i do...
how would i be? what would i do?

the conditioned habits in our minds are stubborn and deeply rooted. we may be working on changing or healing negative patterns for years and yet we find ourselves acting them out anyway.

don't be too hard on yourself when you notice this.

just keep noticing it.

keep observing it.

awareness is key to this process, as our habitual behavior is what we act out unconsciously.

be kind and patient with yourself in this process.

just notice your patterns, accept them, and continue to work toward what is most harmonious and aligned with the truth you know in your heart.

when someone hurts us, we need to realize that it is
because this person is hurting inside.

they are only projecting their pain outward.

what may appear as anger, abuse, or mistreatment on
the surface, is really a deeper cry for help. this does
not mean that they are justified in their actions, but it
means that they are only human, and they suffer just
like we do.

recognizing this we can have true compassion for that
person, and can see beyond their projected actions,
and can give them our love.

by recognizing the truth that all words and actions
reflect a deeper level of a person's state of being, we
can see beyond the mere appearances of chaos,
violence, and destruction, and can see the deeper level
of suffering that lies at the root. By recognizing this
we develop compassion, patience, and love for others,
as we can see a reflection of our own suffering within
them.

why is it that so many of us resist silence?
why do we resist a quiet mind?
when there is nothing to do, nowhere to be, why do we rush to fill the gap?
what are we avoiding?
our modern culture and worldview has many historical influences that have shaped it, and many of us are unaware that our personal and individual thoughts are largely a product of collective influence and conditioning.
there is a well known saying by a philosopher named rene descartes, who lived in the seventeenth century.
the saying is, "i think, therefore i am."
this simple statement, from a man with considerable influence on public thought, had a large role in shaping the popular worldview of modern culture.
it influenced human beings to associate their identity with the mind.
this identification with mind did not originate with descartes' philosophy, but it was certainly strengthened by it, and to this day the majority of human beings in modern culture feel that they are the thinker, the "i" thought with its endless mental chattering, fantasies, fears, desires, and so on.
the mind, in this context, is essentially just thought.
thought primarily operates in two fields: the past, and the future.
the truth, however, is that there is only now, only this immediate moment which is always changing, moving, and vibrating.

to be aware of the now, to see reality as it is, we have
to see without our definitions, beliefs, classifications,
and other mental constructs.
in other words, the mind has to be quiet.
it has been said, "muddy water is best cleared by
being left alone."
when the mind is quiet, reality reveals itself, as it is
ever present.
when we equate our existence with the mind, we fear
mental silence, as we subconsciously feel it is
equivalent to death.
as a result, we are out of touch with reality, and out of
touch with our true nature.
what remains when the mind has become empty and
silent?
what lies beyond the surface of thought?
when you discover this ever-present awareness, and
know it to be your essential self, you will discover
freedom from the mind and its projected problems,
and consequently you will discover the source of real,
unconditional peace.

what is love?
we use the word so often, but do we know what it
really means?
so many of us are looking for love,
but do we know what we are really seeking?
are we looking for security?
for entertainment?
for acceptance?
for someone to give us pleasure,
to satisfy our desires,
or to help us escape our loneliness?
is that what ove is?

you say you love your partner,
and in that love is involved pleasure—the pleasure of
sex,
of having someone to keep you company,
someone to relate to,
someone to distract you from yourself.
you depend on your partner to provide all of these
things for you,
and the moment they fail to do this,
the moment they turn away from you,
or get bored and leave for someone else,
your whole emotional balance is destroyed,
and this disturbance causes jealousy, attachment,
sorrow, pain, fear, anger and so on.
is this love?
is love depending on someone else to satisfy your
desires?

is there a love that is beyond dependence on
something external?
because of our misunderstanding of love,
we seek for our opinion of love in another,
and this love has in it emotional insecurity, fear,
dependence, anxiety, and so on.
so in reality, there is no love present.
for love is not rooted in fear, in possessiveness, in lust
or desire.
love is unconditional,
it is always free,
understanding,
welcoming,
open,
appreciative,
accepting of all.
love judges none,
    but sees all as one,
all as family,
all as self.
this is real love,
and in this love there is total freedom,
both for oneself and for another.
there is no possession, attachment or jealousy,
just genuine care and compassion.
fear is what closes our hearts to others,
and creates a barrier between us and the world.
but true love has no fear, has no barrier.
it is always open and accepting.

i do not care for the love that is associated with
longing, with attachment, dependence, insecurity, and
fear.
i choose to live in the freedom of real love,
where all beings are accepted and respected as they
are.
love is within you,
and when you realize this love within yourself,
you can share it with all beings.
this is the love that i have discovered,
and i welcome you to meet me here.

in the moment when every last identification of consciousness with some object or concept has ceased, there comes forth from unknown depths a state of awareness which is absolutely free, a state of pure and absolute being in which reality is experienced as whole, undivided, and inseparable from oneself.

every being wishes to be happy and free of suffering, but not every being knows the simple art of how to be happy.

most people seek for happiness in external objects and temporary sense pleasures,

thinking that their happiness comes from things outside of themselves.

but it is a simple and undeniable truth that happiness comes from within.

an emotion is a state of being, it is something that we feel within ourselves.

external things often trigger certain internal emotions, but our reactions to external stimulus are conditioned by our memories and past experiences.

this conditioning determines the way that we perceive things to be, and how we choose to respond to certain objects of our experience.

ultimately, happiness is all a matter of perception.

there are people that are happy with very little material things or opportunities for exciting experiences.

there are people who are miserable with material abundance and all the worldly freedom they could ask for.

the truth is that it really doesn't matter what we have or don't have, it just depends upon how we choose to feel with what we have.

can we appreciate the simple joys of life?
can we be relaxed and at peace within ourselves?
can we accept whatever life brings and not resist or
complain?
there is an infinite source of bliss within each one of
us, but only you can tap into this inner bliss.
if you can relax this mind that is ever seeking external
satisfaction, and appreciate the very moment in which
you are living, then contentment is sure to flower
within you.
you are the source of your happiness.
discover the treasure of contentment within you,
and allow yourself to enjoy this beautiful life in peace.

what any desire essentially aims at is a state of non-desire.

we seek to reach fulfillment, to no longer demand anything,

to be completely satisfied.

what we don't realize is that we are seeking a state of being,

and any state of being already exists within us and does not require anything outside of ourselves to attain.

when we seek for true fulfillment in sensory pleasure, we are basing the object of pleasure as the source of our fulfillment, causing us to no longer be fulfilled from the source that already resides within us.

this leads to a continuous cycle of pleasure and pain as the impermanent objects we cling to come and go, or no longer provide us with the satisfaction they once did. to find lasting fulfillment—a state of non-desire—we must return to the source within us.

when we are in-tune with our source, we will be content with simply being, and everything that comes in our lives is appreciated but not needed.

clinging to any object outside of yourself will eventually cause emotional suffering, since all things in the material world are changing and impermanent.

when we are in tune with our source we are at peace. we only lose our peace when we allow our mind to draw us away from our source.

this source is always present within you, you just have to realize it, feel into it, and return to it.

be inwardly silent.
when the mind is empty of thought,
reality reveals itself.

when we are unaware of our mind,
we are constantly distracted by thought,
constantly feeding some imaginary story,
and constantly trying to validate and improve the
image mind has created of ourselves,
the image that most people identify with as "me," or
"i," along with all "my" problems, worries, dreams,
desires, fears, etc.
but "me" is just a word.
"i" is just a thought.
it exists in the mind only, as do all of its memories,
ideas, and stories.
what lies beyond the mind is our natural awareness,
our witnessing presence, which is always here, and is
inherently free from all of the thoughts that arise and
disappear within it.
it is like the open sky.
just as clouds never affect the nature of the sky,
thoughts never effect our true nature.
we only become disturbed when we identify with the
thoughts, when we have interest in them, and mistake
them to be reality.
but if we realize we are the open awareness that sees
all thoughts, we can simply just let thoughts go,
and open ourselves fully to this moment.
most are afraid to do this, because there is a sense of
safety and security in the mind, but this security is
illusory.
it doesn't really exist.
it only prevents you from being free here and now.

just let go, be here, be open, and be present to life.
if you can do this, you'll discover a natural ease to life,
an effortless way of living, where there is no need to
worry or force things, but instead you can just be,
and you can have contentment with things as they are,
and enjoy life in its simple beauty.
this peace is available to everyone at every moment,
if only we can bring awareness to our minds,
and can let go of the thoughts that disturb us
and distract us from the natural joy of living.

how can you see with the eyes of love
when the mind is clouded by judgment?

how is my innermost awareness different from the
innermost awareness of you, or of any other human,
animal, or living being?
having no form, what is there to compare?
are there even many different awarenesses,
or is it only one awareness, which experiences
through many different bodies and circumstances?
the true recognition of our unity in consciousness
results in an intimate sense of love for all life.
once you see your true self in all,
then hatred for others becomes impossible.
for there are no others, there is only one of us.
one life energy, one consciousness, one universe.
the one expresses itself as many, and in this way, it
experiences and discovers its own infinite potential.
we are many, and we are one.
we are unique and different,
and we are also ordinary and the same.
trying to understand this intellectually
brings confusion.
realizing it within your own heart and mind
brings freedom.

the mind is always inviting us to entertain its fantasies
and endless projections.
unconsciously, we continually accept this invitation
and follow the mind where it leads us.
be aware of the mind as it invites you down a path of
thought and choose instead to just stay.
rest in your own nature, your own awareness,
and watch the mind.
soon the play of mind will become apparent,
and you will gain confidence in abiding in your
natural state.

you are that which sees but cannot be seen,
that which hears but cannot be heard,
that which knows but cannot be known.
see this clearly.
give up identification with objects.
rest as the ever present subject.
be as you are.
relax into the peace of your own being.

desire almost always occurs in relation to our sense perception.

we smell something delicious, then the desire arises for us to eat that.

we see something beautiful, then the desire arises for us to have it around for us to look at.

we hear something pleasant, then the desire to continue listening to it arises, and so on.

if we can become aware of the triggers for our desire, we can develop a sense of control over our desires by realizing it is just the mind grasping at the experience of the senses, and intensifying the desire with mental energy.

the more you dwell on it, the stronger the desire becomes.

if we can recognize it instantly, we can let it go as soon as it arises, as we see it is just the grasping quality of the mind.

the mind is always grasping, always clinging to experience, to fantasies, memories, desires, etc.

be aware of this process within you, and realize that it is only the mind and it's resistance to the present moment that disturbs you.

if you can let go of your resistance, whether it is in the form of grasping or pushing away, then you can be at peace with what is.

everything changes.
all is impermanent.
just relax, and let things change as they must.
contentment is within yourself,
within your very beingness.
as the great sage lao tzu said,
"be content with what you have,
rejoice in the way things are.
when you realize nothing is lacking,
the whole world belongs to you."

the greatest of all deceptions is self-deception.
don't be afraid to look at your own mind honestly.
see what is really within you.
what are you motivated by?
what is the intention behind your actions?
what do you think?
what stories do you tell yourself?
what is the content in your mind?
if we deceive ourselves, we cannot love ourselves.
if we cannot love ourselves, we cannot truly love
another, for as long as we have judgment, hatred,
resentment, etc. within us, it will affect the way we
live, and consequently it will affect all of our
relationships.
freedom from the mind and it's self-created problems
is only possible through awareness.
cultivate the awareness that notices every thought that
arises.
don't try to change anything,
don't push anything away.
just look.
just see.
become aware of what has slipped by in the
unconscious shadows.
bring it all into the light,
and let go of what does not serve.
let go of what stands in the way of your natural
openness to life.

let go of the barriers that prevent love from entering into your heart.
let them go by becoming aware of them,
accepting them,
and forgiving them.
surrender it all.
you don't need the barriers to protect you.
surrender to love, and be free.

the degree to which you allow yourself to be open to the world,
is the degree to which the world will open up to you.
if you do not allow yourself to be at that level of vulnerability, openness, and presence, how can anyone else meet you there?
when you become more loving to others, they feel loved, and in turn they become more loving toward you. it is all a matter of genuine interest and presence. think of any relationship you have—family, friend, partner, pet—that being is living their life,
doing their best to live each day, and you are doing the same. when you engage with them, you can be stuck in your mind, your struggles, your hopes, your interests, etc. and they will be stuck in theirs, and not much real communication will take place.
but if you can take a moments rest from your preoccupations, and can sit with that being and be present with them, you'll see them open up,
you'll see that light within them illuminate,
that light that feels the joy of being acknowledged, being respected, being loved.
take the time to be present with those you love, take the time to listen, to enjoy their company, without any agenda of your own.
when you open yourself to the world, the world opens itself to you,
and the joy of intimate connection flowers—a joy which our hearts all long for.

surrender your attachment to conceptual grasping,
and trust in your own nature,
allow yourself to act spontaneously,
without resistance.
when we do this our mind is free to express itself,
free to act clearly in response to the moment,
and free to behave without clinging,
doubt, or mistrust in oneself.

the true masters, no matter where they may reside, always instruct us to look inward—
pointing toward that which is absolute and true, and away from that which illusory and false.
a universal teaching, found throughout all great traditions, no matter what their cultural medium of expression may be, is that our true nature is one with the whole of existence, and since that which is true is always true, it is who we are right here and now.
there is nothing we need to attain, nothing we need to add to ourselves to be who we already are. rather, it is a journey of letting go, of seeing clearly into the very essence of who we are, and being able to shed away the layers and layers of illusion and false identifications that veil us from our essential nature.
in the modern world, we have the idea of becoming, of achieving, of accumulating more.
but the journey of awakening is not so much one of becoming, nor one of gaining.
it is a journey of unbecoming everything we have been conditioned and trained to be, one of releasing all we think we are so that all that remains is our true nature in all its wholeness.
the journey is not one of becoming, but one of being, one of embodying the truth of who we are, opening ourselves up to life and to this moment, being here and now, as we are, completely.
for who we are in our very beingness is the essential nature of existence.

when we are simply being, we are expressing the
universal activity itself.
yet our minds limit us with thoughts of smallness,
thoughts of lack, thoughts of victimhood etc.
can you cultivate the awareness that observes these
thoughts as they arise?
and can you let them go?
can you go deeper into that awareness that sees the
thoughts?
what is that?
it has no name, no form, no culture, no religion.
it simply is, always present, aware, and whole.
it is the ground of being, and it can only be known by
looking within and realizing it as your essential being.

space allows everything to be as it is,
it allows everything to exist within it,
but it is never affected by what exists within it,
it always remains spacious, open, and free.
in the same way, we do not need to destroy thoughts,
just practice being mindful of each moment,
including the thoughts that arise within your mind,
and do not grasp at anything.
when we cling to thought, or try to push it away,
we are resisting the perpetual flow of the present
moment.
by letting go, being open, and remaining present,
we are in touch with reality,
at one with the ever-changing flow,
and free to be at peace with whatever arises.

non-resistance, non-action (effortless action), and
non-thinking (present moment awareness), are
principles revered by the eastern sages.
these masters point directly to the mind,
and remind us to be aware of its subtle nature.
the mind shapes everything, and if we allow ourselves
to be confused by it,
it will create endless problems for us.
wake up from the dream of the mind,
and realize the peace that is here now,
in the reality of this very moment.

when we think we "know" something by means of
intellectual knowledge that we have accumulated
through study, through memory, etc. it is dead
knowledge, it is knowledge of the past.
it cannot help us be in tune with the direct experience
of the present moment.
for the present moment is always changing, and
therefore it is always unknown.
it is living.
to try to capture it in words and concepts is useless
and creates a block between us and reality.
just let go of the need for intellectual understanding
of the truth, and open yourself completely to the
truth of this moment.
when your mind is quiet,
truth reveals itself in all its glory.
it is ever present, here and now.

truth is found in silence,
in presence,
in awareness of the direct experience of life.
this living energy that makes up all things,
including you, is itself the one truth.

reality is simply what is,
here and now,
and when we relax our mind and open up to this
moment,
we see the beauty in it,
we see the living quality of it,
and we see we are not separate from it—nothing is.
all of our problems—our fears, our worries, our
anger, our sadness, our anxiety, etc.—
where do they exist but within the mind?
in this moment, here and now, there is only peace,
only freedom, only unity.
what is beyond the mind?
what is present when the mind is quiet?
there is simply being, simply awareness,
ever present, free, alive, here and now.

a journal entry written after an ayahuasca ceremony:

it was such a familiar feeling.
it is both extremely profound,
yet simple and ordinary at the same time.
it is as if it is obvious that i am always this connected,
yet for some reason it is not always felt
on such a strong level.

i could feel the presence of spirit everywhere,
the formless space beyond every form,
the energy that every form is made of,
and everything in between.
i felt it as the true self in me,
and as everything surrounding me.

everything around me was just vibrations of energy,
and the space was filled with various geometric forms,
all dancing in harmony.

i felt so much unity and bliss.
i laughed at the fact that i could ever forget the spirit
when it is always so universally present.
i laid down and basked in the love and beauty
as i listened to the sweet melody of the icaros.

sitting here, relaxed,
mind is open and spacious like the sky.
thoughts, sounds, and other sensations
come and go—each one just a passing cloud.
how long have i mistaken myself for what i am not?
how long have i sought my identity in these passing
clouds, forgetting that i am the ever-present sky?
how could i overlook something so simple?
how could i forget who i am,
when i am always present?
how much suffering have i caused myself
by grasping at clouds,
hoping to find something lasting
in what is transient by nature?
all appearances come and go.
they arise and dissolve spontaneously.
yet they are always appearing to someone,
to something.
the awareness that sees, can never be seen.
looking for it in the mind and its appearances is like
looking for water in an empty bottle.
yet still we seek,
when what we are looking for is that which is seeking.
the sun can never be aware of its own light,
unless there are objects that can reflect that light.
so too, can awareness not be aware that it is, except
for when there are objects to reflect its presence.
yet the objects are not separate from the subject,
they are two sides of the same coin.
the clouds are not separate from the sky,
yet the sky is not limited to the clouds.

waves are not separate from water,
yet water is not limited to waves.
thoughts are not separate from awareness,
yet awareness is not limited to the mind.
do not look for your true nature in what is only a
fraction of your being.
become aware of that which you are,
which is awareness itself—
the space in which all arises.
allow everything to be as it is.
things come and go as they please.
change is the nature of life,
yet as awareness you are beyond all change.
no matter what happens, you are beyond it.
doubt, questions, uncertainty—
these are states of mind.
who do these states appear to?
what can you be sure of other than that you are?
so allow yourself to be as you are.
end the self-created struggle.
rest in the peace of your own being.
realize you are already free.

life is temporary.

and during this precious time alive, what do we do?

we run around in circles, chasing after desires, pleasure, ambitions, fame, fortune, and so on, hoping this will bring us happiness.

but what is that fortune worth at the moment of death?

where is that security you so desperately sought after?

how will that nice house or that expensive car help you in that fateful moment?

why do we spend so much time chasing after material things, grasping at objects to bring us happiness?

what happiness can we find in such things when they are impermanent?

when our very attachment to them causes our own misery?

is this what life is really worth?

a nice job, nice things, the illusion of security?

we are confused by the mind and all of its desires, hopes, and fears, and we let this fearful mind control and direct our actions.

it thinks of the past, reminiscing on how great it was.

it thinks of the future and of the promise of happiness it will find there.

but it so easily overlooks the peace that is here now, in this sacred moment.

in this moment, there is no need for public approval, for a promise of temporary security, for nice objects or any of the things we spend so much time chasing after.

in this moment all is well,
all is whole and complete, perfect just as it is.
but as long as we are distracted by the mind,
as long as we believe in the thoughts
that come and go endlessly,
and identify our existence with those thoughts,
then they will continue to blind us from this moment,
and they will continue to create our pain.
how foolish these thoughts are, how unnecessary,
how illusory—yet when we believe them to be true,
how destructive, how damaging, how serious they can
seem.
must we use thought to discover that which is beyond
thought?
or can we drop the whole mess of thoughts all
together through the directness of our own
awareness?
can we cultivate the mind that recognizes every
thought that arises, and does not act on them, but
simply lets them dissolve of their own accord?
can we let go of our attachment to thoughts, to self,
to everything impermanent and ungraspable?
can we come back home to the simplicity of being,
and to the peace of this moment?

on the inner journey,
we are observing the mind,
becoming aware of all the subtle patterns,
thoughts, beliefs, concepts and conditioned behaviors
that arise.
during this process, there are often things that come
up that we don't like.
we see the anger we carry, the judgment, the jealousy,
the insecurity, the craving, the attachment, the
perversion, the fear, the trauma, and so on.
we see these inner disturbances and we often feel that
they shouldn't be there,
that they are wrong in some way, and so we judge
ourselves for having them,
and through this self-judgment we create the feeling
of shame.
shame and judgment prevents us from looking further
at this mental content,
and becomes a big road block on the journey within.
we can overcome this block by learning to look at our
minds with compassion and understanding.
we have been conditioned our whole lives, by a
culture that has been conditioned for thousands of
years, and the fact that we are willing to stop in the
midst of this chaos and observe our own minds for
the sake of freedom, love and awakening, is a
powerful and beautiful thing.

meditation and self-inquiry are some of the most
challenging practices one can engage in,
because we come face to face with all of our stuff,
and we have to look at it honestly.
there is no room for self-deception if one wants to go
far on this path.
so be kind towards yourself, look at your conditioned
mind not with judgement,
but with understanding, with care, and with
compassion,
as if you were nurturing a damaged plant back to
health.

rest as the open sky,
allowing all the clouds to be as they are,
letting them come,
letting them go.
just be your natural self,
completely relaxed and free.

how long have i confused my own projections as a
true reflection of reality?
how long have i believed my mind's perception to be
the truth?
how long have i confused illusion with reality?
everyone's experience is relative to their perception—
to their mind's filters of beliefs, judgments, past
experiences and conditioning.
there's an old indian tale that describes a man walking
along a trail at dusk, when suddenly he sees a snake.
he panics, he feels an overwhelming sense of fear, and
he imagines all kinds of ways to deal with this
problem.
"should i run?"
"should i turn around?"
"should i kill it?"
all these thoughts run through his mind,
when finally he decides to craft a torch to light his
path and approach the snake,
only to discover that the snake was nothing but a
rope in the middle of the trail.
this story describes the way in which our projections
deceives us.
our mind projects and we react to these projections as
if they are reality.
but to what extent does this projecting power of the
mind deceive us?
is there even a reality beyond our perception?
how could we know?
who would perceive it?

realizing appearances have no inherent substance, that all are impermanent and perceived according to individual perception, it seems the only thing we can say about reality is that there is an awareness fundamental to every experience—a dreamer for every dream.

in this world of phantoms and changing forms, what always remains is the formless presence of awareness. as the great teacher kalu rinpoche said,

"we live in illusion and the appearance of things. there is a reality. we are that reality.
when you understand this, you see that you are nothing, and being nothing, you are everything.
that is all."

we have invested so much emotion and energy in things that aren't inherently real, taking it all to be so serious.

once we realize we've been deceived by the mind, we may feel a bit ridiculous.

it is as another great sage longchenpa once said

"since everything is but an apparition, having nothing to do with good or bad, acceptance or rejection, one may well burst out in laughter!"

every trigger, every emotional reaction,
 every mental irritation, is a teacher,
pointing the way to our own inner disharmony.
learn from your triggers, see why there is disturbance,
where does it come from, what is the source?
whatever we experience outwardly,
reflects our internal perception.
allow obstacles to be your teacher,
bringing to light that which lies in the shadow.

in the pursuit of learning, working, growing,
achieving, seeking,
or whatever it is you are moving towards,
just remember to enjoy the journey.
don't overlook the beauty of
what is already here and now.
remember to be present.

the mind is constantly moving,
running about, thinking, planning, fantasizing,
worrying, fearing, seeking, desiring, memorizing,
regretting, reflecting, repeating.
hardly ever is the mind quiet and still, here and now
awake to this moment in all its beauty and simplicity.
the mind finds great unease in the present moment,
because when one is simply being in the present
moment, the mind is silent.
fearing silence, fearing the unknown,
the mind seeks for an escape,
it looks for a distraction,
it looks for entertainment,
it looks for drama,
it creates problems,
it creates pressure,
it repeats thought patterns.
the seemingly endless activity of the mind veils us
from the reality of the moment,
and instead we live in a world of mental fantasy and
illusion.
what lies hidden in this moment,
when the mind is quiet and still,
is the intelligence of the heart,
with wisdom that knows far more than the mind
could imagine.
the heart is an organ of perception,
it takes in information from the energetic fields of
everything around it,
responds with an emotional sense,

which, if we are receptive,
can guide us properly in every moment of life.
the mind is a beautiful instrument,
but it is far too stimulated.
without connection to the wisdom of our heart,
the mind becomes clouded with thoughts.
notice how the mind always wants to escape the
moment.
teach the mind to stay.
allow the mind to be quiet.
train yourself to be here now,
to find contentment in simply being,
and to know that this moment is enough.
the endless seeking, worrying, desiring, planning, etc.
is only preventing you from seeing clearly what is here
and now,
and from listening to the wisdom of your heart's
intelligence.
take the time to sit,
to be still,
to observe your mind,
to stay in this moment,
and to let go of all the mental illusions.
truth is here now,
but we cannot be aware of it when our minds are
distracted.
still your mind so that it may reflect the truth.
empty your cup so that it may be filled.
discover what is truly here when the mind is silent.

how often do we take for granted the beauty, the vastness, and the mystery of this existence?

we speak of awareness, of consciousness, spirit, soul, god, divinity, etc. but in our search for intellectual understanding we often fail to appreciate just how incredible all of this is.

you are alive. you are aware. you exist!

how incredible!

so what if you don't know what you are doing, where you're going, why things are this way or that, and so on.

embrace the mystery,

see the beauty in it all,

appreciate the fact that you are alive!

this moment now is enough.

the whole thing is ultimately unknowable anyway.

look at anything in the space around you,

realize that you could zoom into that thing and infinite worlds would reveal themselves.

within your finger,

a strand of hair,

or a drop of rain,

infinite worlds wait to be discovered.

full of beauty, full of life, full of mystery, full of vibration and change.

all of it unknowable by intellectual means.

the common conception of knowledge is that it is a static thing.

when you "know" some "thing" what you "know"

and the "thing" you know are thought to be static and unchanging.

but this is not how reality is.

reality is always changing, on every scale, making it impossible to truly "know" a "thing" because what you know and the thing you "know" are always changing.

yet, there is an interesting question posed to us by the ancient sages.

"what is the one thing that can be known, through which all else becomes known?"

similarly, they have asked, "in a world of constant change, what is that which remains changeless?"

looking within ourselves and asking these questions, we see that everything is changing—thoughts, ideas, beliefs, likes, dislikes, interests, sensations, etc.

what is it that is beyond change?

what is the one thing that is actually knowable about myself?

the only thing i can say, without a doubt, is that i am.

i am alive. i am aware.

existence, my very beingness, the simple fact that I am, and that life is, are the only things i can ever know with certainty.

no matter what happens, as long as there is experience, there is the consciousness that experiences.

how fascinating this awareness
we so casually speak of.

the mind veils reality with its judgments,
discriminations,
labeling,
conceptualizing,
fantasizing,
and endless thinking—
none of which are capable of representing the truth.
to become aware of the true reality we must quiet our
minds, and cultivate awareness of the moment,
feeling it, acting consciously, moving with
mindfulness. in doing so, we become available to life,
rather than being distracted by our own mind and its
noise. with mindfulness, we are aware of what is here
and now, and so, we are then most capable of
responding to what occurs in each moment with
awareness, calmness, stability, and sensibility—
rather than running on auto-pilot reacting out of
conditioning and habitual patterns.
moving with life as it moves,
understanding what is true in each moment,
and knowing how to respond to life intelligently
requires mindful attention.
the mind creates an illusory reality,
and dwelling primarily in the mind is like living in a
dream. mindfulness is the way to awaken from this
dream, and become aware of reality as it truly is.

the mystery that is this natural living world,
has been attempted to be defined by many cultures,
many philosophies, many stories, concepts and
ideologies, continually changing throughout the ages.
yet nature itself remains ever free from the stories
humans create to define it.

nature does not live in the world of language,
concepts, or thought (except through the medium of
human beings which are indeed an expression of
nature).

perhaps imposing philosophies and ideologies onto
nature has only separated us from it.

perhaps the best way to understand nature is not
through verbal description, but through lived
experience.

attentive to our direct experience of the natural world
and its energies, from moment to moment, we can
understand far more than ideology will allow.

when we hold a fixed position, we exclude all other
possibilities.

letting go of all beliefs, we can then become open to
the reality of what is.

when we experience a plant, without clinging to the
idea that it is a plant, a shrub, a flower, or any other
human-made classification, we are able to access
infinite worlds of magic, activity, and mystery that are
unavailable to us when we think we "know" what it is
we are experiencing.

don't be so quick to judge or label something,
whether it is a situation, a person, a plant, or anything
in your experience.
just remain open, aware, and attentive, and the truth
that lies beyond judgment will reveal itself.
many people seek for truth,
yet they are looking for something that will fit their
expectation, and their ideas of what they believe truth
to be.
the truth is right here, available to you now and
always.
make your mind an empty vessel,
and the truth will be given a space to fill.

right now, you are alive.
right now, you are breathing.
right now, you are free.

the past is gone.
it exists only in memory.
the future has yet to come.
it is the great unknown.
but right now, you are here.
here on this earth.
here to experience the mystery of life.
here to share this land with all who inhabit it.
here to choose how you wish to be.

in this moment, all things are possible.
in this moment, all beings share this breath.
in this moment, lies the key to happiness,
freedom, and peace.

words, language, labels, descriptions, definitions, categories, inches, meters, pounds, hours, names, numbers, symbols, signs, concepts, and other human-made measurements are useful tools,

but they can never amount to reality as it truly exists, beyond the confines of human-made symbols and measurements.

we are so fascinated by the world of measurement, that we mistake it for being the actual reality. thus, we feel uncomfortable about a thing if we cannot name it, define it, or categorize it in some way.

as a culture, we have to agree upon these labels and definitions, and also what the "thing" is that we are labeling or defining.

in doing so, we create a "something" by dividing it from the inseparable everything.

we see a "tree" and we agree that it begins at its "roots" and ends at its "leaves," is fed by the "sun," "rain," and "soil," which depends upon "oxygen," "nitrogen" and other "elements," and in this process of naming, we are breaking apart and mentally dividing what is essentially one undivided whole.

not only that, our words give the impression that the things they define are static.

they are either "nouns" or "verbs," but whatever is a noun is itself a verb, as everything is always in motion, and there is no static unchanging "thing."

words and language, as useful of tools as they are,
have given us the impression that we know nature
because we have given it names,
dissected it, and placed its parts into verbal categories.
this is superficial knowledge however, and is only
relevant to our human minds, but is not the actual
truth of nature.
as the philosopher alan watts would say,
"you cannot drink the word water, or eat the word food,"
so too are we unable to truly understand life by trying
to fit it into our limited language, definitions, and
mental constructs.

we are constantly taking in information, more so now
than ever due to the internet and the abundance of
advertisements, commercials, media, etc.
this constant stimulation causes the mind to be
extroverted,
always focused on the continual stimulus that is
flooded through the senses.
because of this, not many people are in touch with
their true nature—
the being that lies beneath the thoughts and
sensations.
the mind is like a lake.
when the water is disturbed by wind, movement, and
other activity, we can't see beyond the surface.
but when the mind is still, like clear water it allows us
to peer into the depths, and to observe what lies
beneath the surface.
alan watts once said,
"muddy water is best cleared by being left alone."
so too, does our true nature become clear to us when
we leave the mind alone, and allow the mind to
become still and quiet.
this allows us to touch the awareness that is beyond
the mind.
instead of focusing on the objects of perception,
we touch the nature of ourselves as the being
that is perceiving.
only, we cannot truly be in touch with our true nature
when the mind is overstimulated, anxious and
distracted.

we need to take some time to stop, relax, and let ourselves be.

rest in mental silence and see what lies beyond the activity of the mind.

what remains when the mind is quiet?

give your mind a break from the constant stimulation, and let yourself rest in your own nature.

there is an incredible feeling of contentment available to you in each moment, when you realize that simply being alive, right here and now, is more than enough reason to be happy.

when you discover the contentment of simply being, then you discover a peace that you can take with you no matter where you go, and no matter what is happening in your external circumstances.

peace is not dependent upon circumstances, but is determined by your inner state of being.

you can be at peace in any situation, simply by allowing things to be as they are, and resting in the contentment of your own existence.

however we cannot reach this level of contentment when we are dependent upon external factors for happiness, and are not in touch with who we are.

wakefulness and moment-to-moment attention to reality makes one sensitive to life, and provides a feeling of intimacy with all things.

there is profound peace and joy to be found in simple daily activities when we are able to engage life with presence.

rather than having a mind that is racing, judging, seeking, etc.

which is common in our modern society,

practice to quiet the mind,

free the mind,

and empty the mind to rest as pure awareness, present to all that is. when the mind is empty, it is available to everything. only when the mind is empty, can it be filled with life's beauty.

to live in a state of not-knowing,

to have a beginner's mind,

means that we are constantly learning about life,

only we are not accumulating knowledge and storing it as memory.

instead we are simply open, attentive and receptive to the flow of life,

and allow ourselves to flow with life effortlessly,

because we do not cling to thoughts, views, beliefs, or experiences. thus when the mind is quiet, and our attention is fully engaged in the moment,

we can find profound peace, joy, awe and mystery in something as simple as peeling potatoes.

aware of awareness itself,
we are absorbed in the bliss of our own being,
free from the projections of the mind,
in touch with reality as it truly is.

i have been a seeker of truth for a long time.
i have looked for truth in books,
i have looked for it in travel,
i have looked for it in relationships.
but i have realized that truth is not a static,
unmoving thing.
the truth is living,
it is dancing and changing constantly.
truth is like a river,
it flows, it moves, it carries life with it.
and just like truth,
we are not static lifeless things,
but we too are alive,
constantly moving, flowing, and changing.
to seek for truth somewhere else,
somewhere outside of ourselves,
only prevents us from finding the living truth
that exists within us.
to discover the truth of life,
allow yourself to be filled with the truth,
simply by letting yourself be open to your direct
experience,
and embracing all that arises with full acceptance and
heart centered presence.
welcome everything, no matter what it is.
we've become so removed from our direct experience
of life,
so closed off and separated,
because most of us are so distracted by our minds and
our constant mental chatter.

our minds are full of noise, full of worry, full of
doubt, full of fear, limiting beliefs and so on.
because of this, we overlook the living reality of this
moment.
we feel as if we are separate observers,
who can stand apart from life,
analyze it, dissect it and pick it apart.
but in truth, there is no separation in nature.
only our minds can believe in the illusion of
separation,
yet things are always and have always been one
undivided whole.
to reconnect with the fullness of life,
let your mind be quiet,
and let your heart be open.
open your senses.
open your awareness.
start feeling the world,
start really exploring the energy constantly pouring in
through your sensory doorways.
our senses were formed and shaped by our evolution
in nature,
and so our senses can connect us directly to nature,
because the senses always operate in the present
moment.
so to help quiet the mind and become fully present to
life,
start reconnecting to your direct sensory experience—
without labeling it, judging it,
or conceptualizing it in any way.

to have a goal is a great source of motivation and
purpose, and it certainly requires a lot of focus and
effort to bring those immaterial plans,
ideas, and visions into physical form.
but if we focus too much on our goals,
too much on what we desire,
it becomes a source of suffering.
we become anxious, stressed, pressured, perhaps
doubtful, worried, or who knows what else.
in this process, we overlook the reality of what's
actually here and now, a reality in which really all is
well, and in which the only thing that disturbs our
peace is our own minds.
remember that your mind is the source of your
greatest suffering, but it can also be the source of
great joy and peace.
if you are caught in a struggle caused by your own
mental conflict, try to see the unreality of it.
you might even want to laugh at the fact that you've
been so immersed in a projection that simply isn't
real. then let it go, relax, and let yourself be.
peace is available here and now.
your goals will come to fruition as long as you hold
that intention and vibration,
and are willing to act on it.
so just relax and trust the process as it unfolds.
all will happen in divine timing

who says there has to be a limit to the amount of joy
we can feel in each moment?
who determines whether we feel happy or sad?
who makes the decision as to what determines our
inner state?
do we need a reason to feel joy or can we choose to
be joyful for its own sake?
who is in charge of our feelings?
we are the ones that determine our inner state of
being.
it isn't a result of our circumstances.
it isn't determined by what we do or don't have.
it's only a matter of perception, of attitude, of choice.
quiet that noisy and restless mind,
give yourself a break.
the mind wants perfection.
yet nothing could ever amount to the mind's idea of
perfection.
things are already perfect as they are.
so rejoice!
you are alive!
you are breathing in this fresh air and life force!
you are seeing a world of mystery, color and beauty!
a world that is inseparable from you.
you are one with all that is.
you effect all that is.
let go of the struggle,
stop creating problems for yourself.
realize all is well and relax!

let things be.
accept everything just as it is.
embrace the world,
and fall in love with what exists.

connect to the true reality of the world
by letting go of conceptual knowledge
and touching the living essence
of what is here and now.

when we let go of our attachment to any and all
forms of identification,
we stand face to face with the great mystery of life,
the unknowable and ungraspable reality of the here
and now.
fearlessly open your heart and mind to the present
moment,
and stand in this vulnerable presence to what is.
this radical openness to the mystery of life is the soil
in which the flower of love grows.
open and present to all things, without any seeking
for an identity to separate us, we realize our unity with
life and within us grows an incredible intimacy with
every living being,
and every precious moment of our experience

we cannot know reality by thinking about it,
by trying to make it fit into our concepts and
conventions.
we know reality by experiencing reality.
it is so unbelievably simple, that the ego wishes there
was something more.
what we do not realize though, is that when we enter
this state of being that is free from thought,
a whole new universe is experienced,
and in this new universe we experience true freedom,
true joy, and true love for all of existence.

your body and my body are both totally made up of and dependent upon the elements of the earth—the water, the air, the heat, the land, the soil and the food it produces—as well as all of the elements that these elements are dependent upon—the sun, the stars, the galaxies, and a vast field of energy and space to contain them in.

nature is our extended body, and the elements outside of our skin are just as important to our health as the elements within our skin. our bodies are connected to the universe as a whole, and consequently to each other and the many ways in which we influence our shared environment.

when we look at a tree, we do not see the tree for what it really is.
we see how it appears to us on the surface, and we dismiss it as being just another form in the universe. we fail to realize that the tree is connected to the universe on every level; that all of nature is expressing itself through that single form. there can be no tree without the earth that it grows from, the sun that gives it energy, the water that nourishes its growth, and the millions of fungi and bacteria fertilizing its soil. looking deeply into anything in nature, we realize that it is connected to the whole. we see that nature is one seamless web, and the notion that things have an existence of their own is merely an illusion.

the suffering of the world is a reflection of the
suffering that exists within the minds of human
beings. we are at war with ourselves,
and so we create war with others.
until we are at peace with our own being,
we cannot be at peace with others, or with nature.
the root of all our problems are within the mind,
and so they can also be solved within the mind.
when we choose to stop seeing ourselves as victims of
the world,
we are called to take responsibility for ourselves and
how we impact the world.
in doing so, we must acknowledge our thoughts and
actions, and realize where there is disturbance. this
inner disturbance affects all of our relationships,
but if we can cultivate peace within ourselves,
then we can bring that peace into the world.
when enough human beings have developed
inner peace, there will be no more war,
no more hatred and violence amongst each other,
and we will be able to truly live in harmony.
but it must start with us.
we must do our part to heal our own conditioning,
and to embody the peace that is needed to
heal our world.

life is our greatest teacher.
every moment holds within it a lesson for our
spiritual growth.
challenging situations give us the opportunity to
practice patience, perseverance, and acceptance.
pleasant situations give us the opportunity to practice
joy, relaxation, and appreciation.
every moment, every event, every situation can be
your teacher if you are open to learning.
when something stirs up an
emotional reaction within you,
what can you learn about yourself?
what can you learn about your triggers, your wounds,
and what needs your attention and healing?
every moment is an opportunity for growth.
you don't need to find a teacher, a guru, or a mentor,
as helpful as they may be at times.
life itself is your greatest teacher.
your heart is your guru.
your intuition is your mentor.
allow everyday life to be your teacher,
and learn from the lessons that it gives to you.
this is the surest and quickest way to grow.

reality is vast, fluid, and ever-present,
containing infinite possibilities that are forever
unfolding in unison.
words, concepts, and thoughts particularize reality,
shifting one's focus on to what is finite,
temporary, and illusory.
words and concepts are only symbols that represent
reality, they are not reality itself.
reality itself is ineffable, unspeakable, and unknowable
by means of conceptual thinking.
one cannot know reality through the intellect,
as it divides and veils reality by its very nature.
to confuse words for reality is like confusing a
mirrored image for the reality it is reflecting.
hence the famous zen saying,
"the teachings are only a finger pointing to the moon."
don't concentrate on the finger alone or you will miss
the true reality it is pointing to.
understand the limits of language
and conceptual thinking.
allow yourself to open to the true reality
that is ever present, here and now.

have you allowed yourself to rest recently?
not just physically, but mentally?
have you taken time out of your day to just relax and
be at peace?
to just be, with no need for doing anything else?
we spend so much time in our minds, thinking,
planning, worrying, fantasizing, regretting, etc.
and in doing so, we neglect the present moment in
which we live.
in this moment, peace is always available when we can
simply allow what is present to be.
if we can relax with what is, no matter what it is, we
can be at peace internally, regardless of external
sensations and circumstances.
in this moment the totality of life is expressing itself.
in this moment all things are coexisting
in a cosmic dance.
in this moment there is no separation between oneself
and "others"
everything just is.
it is all just happening as it is.
and you are a part of this great cosmic happening.
relax your mind and open yourself to
the present moment.
be attentive to what is here.
feel it deeply.
the more we bring our presence into each moment,
the more we free ourselves from the prison of the
mind and our constant mental chatter,
and the more joy, beauty, and vitality we feel.

the present moment enlivens us as we are awake to
the essence and movement of life.
no concepts or intellectual philosophies have any
value here.
here and now everything just is.
allow yourself to just be.
tune in to the mystery and beauty of this present
moment in which all life is happening.

allow what is to be as it is.

in this very moment, how deeply can you let go?
how deeply can you let go of all the fears, the worries,
the regrets, the hopes, the dreams, the concerns.
how deeply can you let go of their weight over you?
how deeply can you let go and enter into the state of
being that is there when everything else has left, that
silent being that is existence itself?
letting go of all mental activity and resting in your
own beingness,
you can find pure contentment,
the contentment and peace of simply being.
let go of what disturbs your mind from resting in its
own nature.
allow yourself to just be.

i know how easy it is to feel like today is just another
day, that days go by feeling like nothing special,
like nothing interesting is happening,
stuck in the same monotonous routine.
but please, try to see the preciousness of life.
try to see the preciousness of each moment.
tomorrow is not promised, to you or to anyone.
what you have now, the people in your life, the things
you enjoy, the state of your health,
it's all so precious.
nothing is permanent, and what seems like it is always
here will one day disappear.
it's easy to overlook the preciousness of life.
but imagine all the things you appreciate,
and imagine if they were to suddenly all disappear at
this very moment,
how would you feel?
well one day they will disappear,
the whole experience of this life will disappear.
so, do not be afraid to let go,
but cherish what you have now while you have it.
cherish your body, cherish your family, your friends,
your interests, what makes you happy.
cherish it all, and be grateful.
it is all temporary, and oh so precious.

your true being is formless ever-present awareness,
the space in which all things exist.

you are like the screen on which the movie of life is
played. many have forgotten their true nature as the
screen, and have identified with the actors and events
that occur within the screen.

just as the screen in which all appearances occur,
remains untouched by those appearances at all times,
your true nature also remains untouched by all
appearances that arise within it.

it is what allows all appearances to be.

remember your true nature.

abide in your eternal formless presence and be free.

whenever you are feeling sad,
feeling lost,
feeling down,
try shifting your focus onto what you have,
onto what you are grateful for—
the air you breathe,
water you drink,
food you eat,
life you live.
there are so many things to be grateful for.

much of the time we live in a fantasy.
we are constantly fantasizing about our future,
our dreams, our goals, our fears, our worries, our
memories, imaginary scenarios that haven't occurred.
it's a beautiful thing that we have imagination,
and that we are able to fantasize, to dream, to plan.
but this can also easily bring us
out of touch with reality.
reality is here and now,
and it is always changing.
it doesn't always change according to our desires,
there are too many factors at play in this
interconnected web of life.
imagination is essential for creation,
so of course there is nothing wrong with fantasies.
but be mindful of when you are fantasizing,
and try not to confuse illusion with reality.
check in with how frequently you fantasize,
and remember to bring yourself back to the present.
all it takes is one breath
to acknowledge your mental fantasy,
and to let it go.
imagination is beautiful,
but life is now.
life is here.
remember to be here,
remember to live now.

don't neglect this precious moment by constantly
fantasizing and planning about the future.
there are countless people, who in their last moments,
said the exact same thing.
only they were saying it with regret for not realizing it
sooner.
life is impermanent.
life is uncertain.
life is precious.
appreciate this life,
and allow yourself to live life fully present
to what is here and now.

i notice so many people wanting to use "spirituality"
as a form of escape from the world,
as a form of security,
as if enlightenment will be our final safe harbor where
we can rest forever.
existence is always moving, always dancing, always
changing.
there is no real security in that.
enlightenment is not security.
it frees us from both security and insecurity.
it teaches us to be fully present to life in all its forms.
it teaches us to accept reality and to dance with it,
as we are not and cannot ever be separate from it.
a true spiritual path does not help us to escape reality.
it helps us to be more fully involved in reality,
yet less attached to our minds ideas of reality.
i know that life can be frightening at times,
that uncertainty can be scary.
but life is uncertain,
and if we are going to live life peacefully we cannot
constantly try to escape it.
we need to find better ways to live with it,
to understand it, to accept it, and to acknowledge our
responsibility in helping to create it.

one of our greatest superpowers
is the ability to choose.
we choose how we wish to think and act.
we choose whether we wish to live in fear or love,
whether we wish to take responsibility
for ourselves or not.
we choose whether we wish to own up to our
experience and embrace the challenges,
or deny them and run away from them.
we choose whether we wish to acknowledge our pain,
our conditioning, our harmful habits, and to heal our
wounds so that we can grow and live better lives,
or whether we wish to hide from these things and
continue to let them govern us subconsciously.
the inner journey is challenging.
facing yourself can be scary.
accepting where you are can be hard.
but it is through awareness of ourselves
that we are able to heal,
able to change, able to grow.
this is what our planet needs:
people who are willing to shine the light of awareness
on the shadows of ignorance in our culture.
we have kept too many things in the shadow:
the violence, the injustice, the racism, the poverty, the
corruption, etc.
we need to bring these things to light so they can heal,
and we have to begin with ourselves.

if a judgment has power over me,
it is because i believe it.
if i don't believe it,
it's power is gone.
no one can make me feel inferior,
unless i agree that i am.
i am the only one that determines
what i believe to be true or untrue,
no one else.

in stressful circumstances,
just remember to pause and breathe!
you don't have to let external situations
affect your inner peace.
stay centered in your breath
and let nature take its course.

life is experience, and through experience we grow.
however, many of us do not fully experience life in
this moment, but instead we occupy far too much of
our time with anticipating future moments, or
clinging to past moments.

the fact that we can conceive of time as past, present,
and future, has certainly worked to our species
advantage, but this conceptualization of time is out of
balance.

we are so accustomed to it that we forget it is only a
concept, only a tool to aid in our survival.

the only true reality is happening in the present.
always.

there is no real past.

there is no real future.

there is only now, and this now is always changing.
it has changed before, it will change again, it is
changing now, as life is change.

what is your relationship with change?

do you fear it?

does it make you feel unstable or insecure?

or do you allow it?

do you embrace it?

do you accept it because you cannot stop it?

without change, there can be no life.

the same change we look forward to at times in our
lives, is the same change we fear and resist at others.

understand the changing and impermanent nature of
reality, and you will be able to truly appreciate
what is here now.

we miss out on the beauty of life now,
because we are lost in our minds,
lost in fantasies, lost in dreams, lost in expectations,
lost in memories.
realize the transient nature of these thought forms,
and just let them go.
bring your attention to the moment.
bring life into your awareness.
don't crave an experience other than this.
what is here now is perfect just as it is.
you are alive, you are breathing, and there is joy in
this simple fact.
even more incredible, you're the entire universe
experiencing itself as a human being.
how incredible is that?
realize your magnificence.
enjoy this life.
die to the past.
do not fear the uncertainty of the future.
trust the course of life.
live now.

you don't have to have it all figured out.
information is endless.
perception is limited.
just be.
this is enough.

take time out of your day to pause and connect with
yourself.
let your mind be still, breathe, and observe what
comes up.
whatever presents itself, let it be there.
if it is a thought, witness it, allow it to come, allow it
to go.
if it is a feeling, feel it completely, then let it go.
take the time to tune into your inner reality,
see what is going on within you.
our inner reality is constantly guiding our thoughts
and actions,
and when we bring it into awareness we are no longer
victims of unconscious influences,
but reclaim our natural freedom to choose how we
wish to live,
how we wish to think, to feel, to be.
this freedom from mental turmoil and unconscious
influence is only possible with mindful presence,
moment to moment awareness of the ever-changing
dance of life.

every meal you eat is mother earth nourishing you,
becoming you, and living through you.
your body is made of earth.
you are earth.
you cannot separate yourself from your environment.
you are and always will be one with the whole of
nature.

whoever you are,
wherever you are,
if you are reading this now,
pause.
take a deep breath in,
and let it go!
whatever it is.
we all carry way too much with us.
thoughts that don't serve us.
judgments.
fear.
worry.
anxiety.
stress.
uncertainty.
sorrow.
regret.
shame.
guilt.
you name it.
whatever it is that is disturbing your peace in this
moment.
pause.
take a deep breath in.
and let it go.
you are okay.
you are enough.
life is beautiful.
don't let your mind blind you
from the beauty in your heart.

a helpful practice can be to ask yourself
when making a decision:

am I affirming life or denying it?
or
am I choosing love or fear?

this can help you make decisions with clarity if your
intention is to choose life and health
over death and sickness,
and love and peace over fear and violence.
every single moment we are at a crossroads between
these choices.
we are either choosing to move closer to our spirit,
or further away from it.

what is fear really, and why does it have so much
influence over us?
there is a difference between danger and fear.
it's good to be aware of when you are in physical
danger, and to avoid that danger.
but most of our fears are not here to protect us from
physical danger,
they were created to protect ourselves socially—
to protect our image, our idea of ourselves,
how others perceive us.
we are so involved in our thoughts that we have
created a whole new dimension of fear that has
nothing to do with our physical survival.
we are now living under the influence of
psychological fear,
fears created by our thoughts that have no basis in
reality.
our minds have created an idea of who we are,
we imagine ourselves to be a certain way,
to be a certain type of person,
and when anything comes along that might challenge
our belief in who we are or what we identify with,
we become afraid, we feel threatened,
because our personal beliefs and ideas about our
identity are being challenged.
most of our fears are subconscious, and so they
influence us without us really being aware
of their presence.
what i have been doing gradually for the past few
years, is noticing when my fears arise,

and then doing the very thing that i am afraid of in that moment.
what i have found is that the reality of a situation is almost never as i was afraid it would be.
i realized that my fears had no basis in reality,
and that they were only limiting me from doing the things i really wanted to do,
and being the person i really wanted to be.
it's really an amazing thing just how resistant we are to facing our fears.
people will spend their entire lives doing something they don't like, to impress people that don't care about them, because they are too afraid to just be themselves and take a chance at doing what makes them happy.
don't let this happen to you.
fear is not a reality.
it is only in the mind.

observe your thoughts.

notice your fears.

inquire into them and ask yourself where they came
from,

what purpose do they serve, and are they true?

if we can look at our fears in this way, we can start to
use fear as one of our greatest teachers, giving us
more insight into our thoughts, our emotions, our
personality, our history, etc.

when fear is our normal state of being,

we have no room to let love in, and without love,

life is unfulfilling and true happiness is not possible.

look at your fears, learn from them, and let them go,

so that you can live a life of love, a life true to who
you are, and a life free from the influence of
unnecessary psychological fears.

it is no secret that life comes with
challenges and suffering.
understanding this can bring compassion
for other living beings.

we all have only a short time together on this planet.
be grateful for the time that is shared.
don't stress over the little things.
do not burden others with your expectations.

just allow yourself the space to be in this moment,
and be kind to every living being
that shares this precious moment with you.

54444195R00097